My Dance Journal

by Megan Bowers

Published by JJ Moffs Independent Book Publisher 2020

JJMoffs Independent Book Publisher Ltd
Grove House Farm, Grovewood Road,
Misterton, Nottinghamshire DN10 4EF

Typeset by Anna Richards
Fashion drawings by Ethan Leyland, Fashion Designer

THIS DANCE JOURNAL BELONGS TO:

Make sure you *Never* give up on your *Dreams*

WELCOME

This is not a book to just look at. It's a creative space for you to write, draw, doodle all over.

Soon it will be your own little catalogue of everything to do with dance. A space where you can record your ideas, share your thoughts, work on yourself and fill it with passion.

Soon it'll be a handmade map that can guide you back to your happiest self, back to your sweet spot in life. Something that you love...

DANCE

4

GOAL SETTING

What are your dreams?

What do you want to achieve
with your dancing?
Have a good think.
Go write...

GOAL SETTING

Think long and hard and use these next few pages to record your goals. 'A goal should scare you a little, & excite you A LOT.'

Short Term Goals
(Write five goals you can achieve within a year)

1

2

3

4

5

GOAL SETTING

Short Term Goals

What are the steps you are going to take to achieve your goals and chase your hopes and dreams? Fill in the clouds with ideas.

GOAL SETTING

'Feel it, see it in your mind's eye, believe it, and most of all- trust that it can be yours...
It has been yours all along.'

Long Term Goals
(Write five goals you can achieve within five years)

♡ 1

♡ 2

♡ 3

♡ 4

♡ 5

GOAL SETTING

Long Term Goals

What are the steps you are going to take to achieve your goals and chase your hopes and dreams? Fill in the clouds with ideas.

INSPIRATION

Who do you look up to?

Have a good think.
I'm sure that's an easy question.
Go write...

DANCE & SET YOUR MIND FREE

INSPIRATION

A true artist is not one who is inspired but one who inspires others.

You can learn so much from watching others. Just by watching you can pick up on so many new skills. You can watch your favourite dancers, pick out what makes them amazing and then apply it to your dance training and performance. Not copy, but just be inspired to help you grow as a dancer and artist. However, never compare your dance journey with someone else's.

It's not a competition or race. It's super hard when you're constantly around people chasing the same dream, but just keep sight of what you want and work hard for you.

INSPIRATION
My favourite dancers

Name:

Age:

Draw photo

Why would you say they're one of your favourite dancers?

What can you learn from them?
And how can you apply that to your dancing/training?

INSPIRATION

My favourite dancers

Name:

Age:

Draw photo

Why would you say they're one of your favourite dancers?

What can you learn from them?
And how can you apply that to your dancing/ training?

INSPIRATION

My favourite dancers

Name:

Age:

Draw photo

Why would you say they're one of your favourite dancers?

What can you learn from them?
And how can you apply that to your dancing/ training?

INSPIRATION
My favourite dancers

Name:

Age:

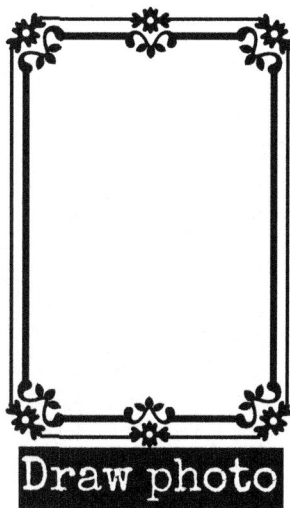
Draw photo

Why would you say they're one of your favourite dancers?

What can you learn from them?
And how can you apply that to your dancing/ training?

INSPIRATION

My favourite dancers

Name:

Age:

Draw photo

Why would you say they're one of your favourite dancers?

What can you learn from them?
And how can you apply that to your dancing/ training?

INSPIRATION
My favourite dancers

Draw photo

Name:

Age:

Why would you say they're one of your favourite dancers?

What can you learn from them?
And how can you apply that to your dancing/ training?

STRENGHTS &WEAKNESSES

What do you need to work on?
What do you slay?

Have a good think.
I'm sure that's an easy question.
Go write...

STRENGTHS & WEAKNESSES

The thing is, every individual is completely different and we all learn differently based on our personalities.

It is crucial to know yourself and your capacities to learn how to progress.

Your strengths give you leverage so you can use them to push yourself further.

On the other hand, your weaknesses are the areas you need to improve on, however this does not mean it's your downfall. It is not something you lack. It is something you need to develop and build, with a little more extra time and hard work.

In order to improve on your weaknesses and advance your strengths you first need to know them.

Fill in the next three pages of all your strengths and weaknesses, so you can always look at this book to remind you what you're good at and what you need to work on!

STRENGTHS	WEAKNESSES

STRENGTHS	WEAKNESSES

STRENGTHS	WEAKNESSES

PLANNER

Getting organised is a sign of self-respect.

A place for everything, and everything in its place.

MY DANCE TIME TABLE

DATES

MONDAY

TUESDAY

WEDNESDAY

THURSDAY

FRIDAY

SATURDAY

SUNDAY

Notes

MY DANCE TIME TABLE

DATES

MONDAY

TUESDAY

WEDNESDAY

THURSDAY

FRIDAY

SATURDAY

SUNDAY

Notes

MY DANCE TIME TABLE

DATES

MONDAY

TUESDAY

WEDNESDAY

THURSDAY

FRIDAY

SATURDAY

SUNDAY

Notes

MY DANCE TIME TABLE

DATES

MONDAY

TUESDAY

WEDNESDAY

THURSDAY

FRIDAY

SATURDAY

SUNDAY

Notes

MY DANCE TIME TABLE

DATES

MONDAY

TUESDAY

WEDNESDAY

THURSDAY

FRIDAY

SATURDAY

SUNDAY

Notes

MY DANCE TIME TABLE

DATES

MONDAY

TUESDAY

WEDNESDAY

THURSDAY

FRIDAY

SATURDAY

SUNDAY

Notes

♡ TO DO LIST ♡

♡ TO DO LIST ♡

♡ TO DO LIST ♡

♡ TO DO LIST ♡

DATES TO REMEMBER

January

....
....
....
....
....
....

February

....
....
....
....
....
....

March

....
....
....
....
....
....

April

....
....
....
....
....
....

May

....
....
....
....
....
....

June

....
....
....
....
....
....

July

....
....
....
....
....
....

August

....
....
....
....
....
....

September

....
....
....
....
....
....

October

....
....
....
....
....
....

November

....
....
....
....
....
....

December

....
....
....
....
....
....

DATES TO REMEMBER

January

February

March

April

May

June

July

August

September

October

November

December

DANCE
WISH LIST

Buy My Dance Journal ☑

☐

☐

☐

☐

☐

☐

☐

DANCE
WISH LIST

☐

☐

☐

☐

☐

☐

☐

☐

WEBSITES TO REMEMBER:

EMAIL ADDRESSES:

PHONE NUMBERS TO REMEMBER:

STUDIO ADDRESSES TO REMEMBER:

FOOD DIARY

MONDAY
BREAKFAST

LUNCH

DINNER

SNACKS

TUESDAY
BREAKFAST

LUNCH

DINNER

SNACKS

WEDNESDAY
BREAKFAST

LUNCH

DINNER

SNACKS

THURSDAY
BREAKFAST

LUNCH

DINNER

SNACKS

FRIDAY
BREAKFAST

LUNCH

DINNER

SNACKS

SATURDAY
BREAKFAST

LUNCH

DINNER

SNACKS

SUNDAY
BREAKFAST

LUNCH

DINNER

SNACKS

NOTES

FOOD DIARY

MONDAY
BREAKFAST

LUNCH

DINNER

SNACKS

TUESDAY
BREAKFAST

LUNCH

DINNER

SNACKS

WEDNESDAY
BREAKFAST

LUNCH

DINNER

SNACKS

THURSDAY
BREAKFAST

LUNCH

DINNER

SNACKS

FRIDAY
BREAKFAST

LUNCH

DINNER

SNACKS

SATURDAY
BREAKFAST

LUNCH

DINNER

SNACKS

SUNDAY
BREAKFAST

LUNCH

DINNER

SNACKS

NOTES

FOOD DIARY

MONDAY

BREAKFAST

LUNCH

DINNER

SNACKS

TUESDAY

BREAKFAST

LUNCH

DINNER

SNACKS

WEDNESDAY

BREAKFAST

LUNCH

DINNER

SNACKS

THURSDAY

BREAKFAST

LUNCH

DINNER

SNACKS

FRIDAY

BREAKFAST

LUNCH

DINNER

SNACKS

SATURDAY

BREAKFAST

LUNCH

DINNER

SNACKS

SUNDAY

BREAKFAST

LUNCH

DINNER

SNACKS

NOTES

FOOD DIARY

MONDAY
BREAKFAST

LUNCH

DINNER

SNACKS

TUESDAY
BREAKFAST

LUNCH

DINNER

SNACKS

WEDNESDAY
BREAKFAST

LUNCH

DINNER

SNACKS

THURSDAY
BREAKFAST

LUNCH

DINNER

SNACKS

FRIDAY
BREAKFAST

LUNCH

DINNER

SNACKS

SATURDAY
BREAKFAST

LUNCH

DINNER

SNACKS

SUNDAY
BREAKFAST

LUNCH

DINNER

SNACKS

NOTES

FOOD DIARY

MONDAY

BREAKFAST

LUNCH

DINNER

SNACKS

TUESDAY

BREAKFAST

LUNCH

DINNER

SNACKS

WEDNESDAY

BREAKFAST

LUNCH

DINNER

SNACKS

THURSDAY

BREAKFAST

LUNCH

DINNER

SNACKS

FRIDAY

BREAKFAST

LUNCH

DINNER

SNACKS

SATURDAY

BREAKFAST

LUNCH

DINNER

SNACKS

SUNDAY

BREAKFAST

LUNCH

DINNER

SNACKS

NOTES

FOOD DIARY

MONDAY

BREAKFAST

LUNCH

DINNER

SNACKS

TUESDAY

BREAKFAST

LUNCH

DINNER

SNACKS

WEDNESDAY

BREAKFAST

LUNCH

DINNER

SNACKS

THURSDAY

BREAKFAST

LUNCH

DINNER

SNACKS

FRIDAY

BREAKFAST

LUNCH

DINNER

SNACKS

SATURDAY

BREAKFAST

LUNCH

DINNER

SNACKS

SUNDAY

BREAKFAST

LUNCH

DINNER

SNACKS

NOTES

BIRTHDAYS
TO REMEMBER

January

July

February

August

March

September

April

October

May

November

June

December

Places you want to go...

Notes

Notes

CLASSES

The best bit about dance.

What classes are beneficial?
What classes make you happy?
Go on tell me. . .

CLASS WISH LIST

Jot down all the choreographers you wish you could take a class with. This could be anywhere in the world, just use your imagination.

YOUR FAVOURITE CLASSES

Who do you love learning from?
What classes do you come away from and feel happy and satisfied?
Who have you learnt a lot from?
Use the next few pages to fill in who and why.

Choreographer:

Why do you enjoy this class?

What do you learn from the class and the teacher?

Choreographer:

Why do you enjoy this class?

What do you learn from the class and the teacher?

Choreographer:

Why do you enjoy this class?

What do you learn from the class and the teacher?

YOUR FAVOURITE CLASSES

Choreographer:

Why do you enjoy this class?

What do you learn from the class and the teacher?

Choreographer:

Why do you enjoy this class?

What do you learn from the class and the teacher?

Choreographer:

Why do you enjoy this class?

What do you learn from the class and the teacher?

YOUR FAVOURITE CLASSES

Choreographer:

Why do you enjoy this class?

What do you learn from the class and the teacher?

Choreographer:

Why do you enjoy this class?

What do you learn from the class and the teacher?

Choreographer:

Why do you enjoy this class?

What do you learn from the class and the teacher?

MAKE UP

Oh, you better get creative, darling...

Think of your dream dance make up,
then create it.
Get your coloured pencils out.

May your
day be as
flawless as
your make up

Over the next few pages, I want you to shade and colour and create some beautiful different make up looks for all different occasions.

Be as creative as you can; think outside the box.

Describe this look, what could this look be used for?

Describe this look, what could this look be used for?

Describe this look, what could this look be used for?

Describe this look, what could this look be used for?

Describe this look, what could this look be used for?

Describe this look, what could this look be used for?

Describe this look, what could this look be used for?

Describe this look, what could this look be used for?

FASHION

Surely this has to be your favourite section...

Imagine you have all the materials in the world in every colour, what would you create?
Doh, obviously a dance outfit or costume!
Get creating the most stylish dance outfits.

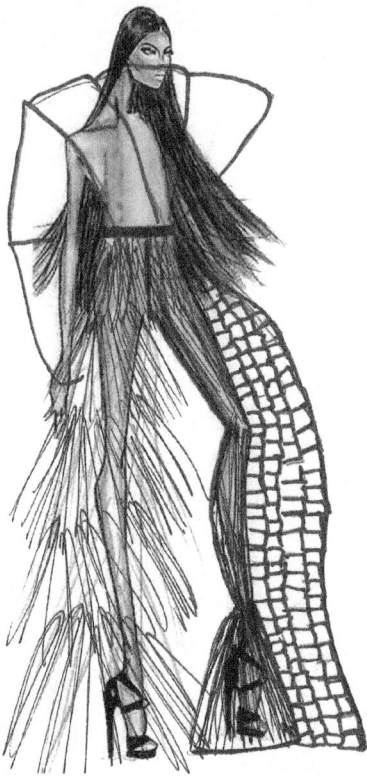

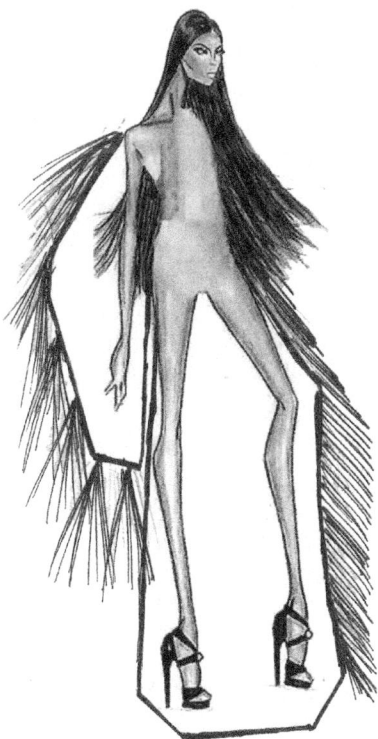

Creativity never goes out of style...

CREATE YOUR OWN

Create your own DANCE WEAR
Create your own SHOW COSTUMES
Create your own COMPETITION SUITS
Create your own STYLE!

I am giving you the platform to live your best life. Imagine you're a fashion designer. Get sketching and creating your fashion ideas for different dance related events. Design and create on the body outlines over the next few pages.

★ TIPS ★

Make sure you sketch your designs in pencil so you can rub them out if you make any mistakes. Once you are happy with your designs then you can start adding colour.

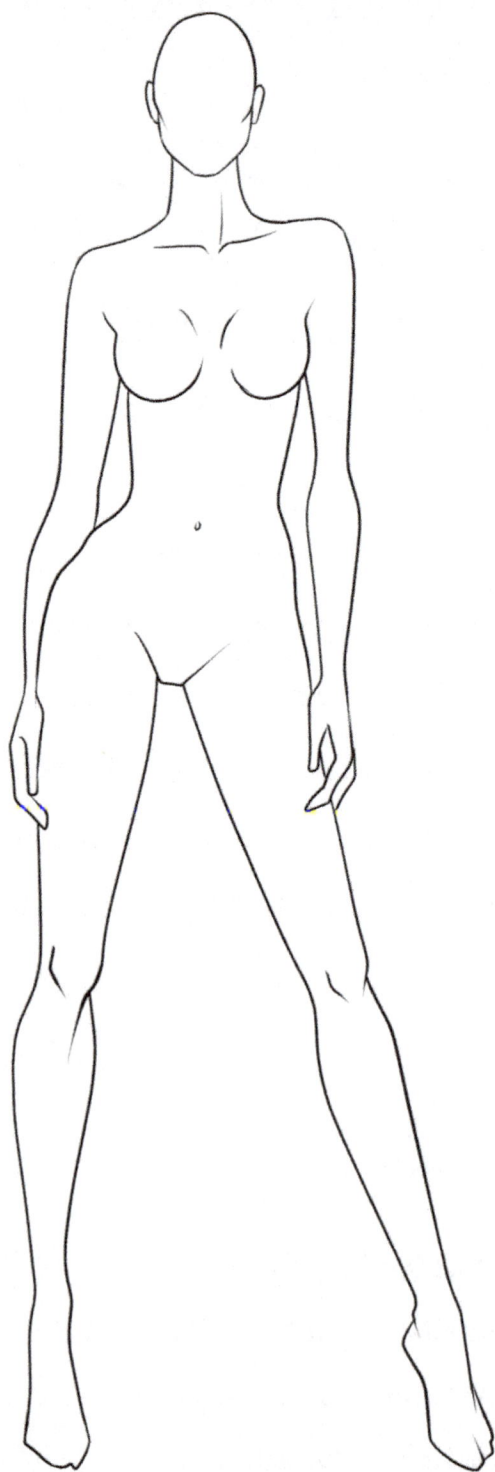

80

WHAT EVENT IS THIS LOOK FOR?

What inspired you for this look?

What kind of materials would you use?

Any other notes describing this look:

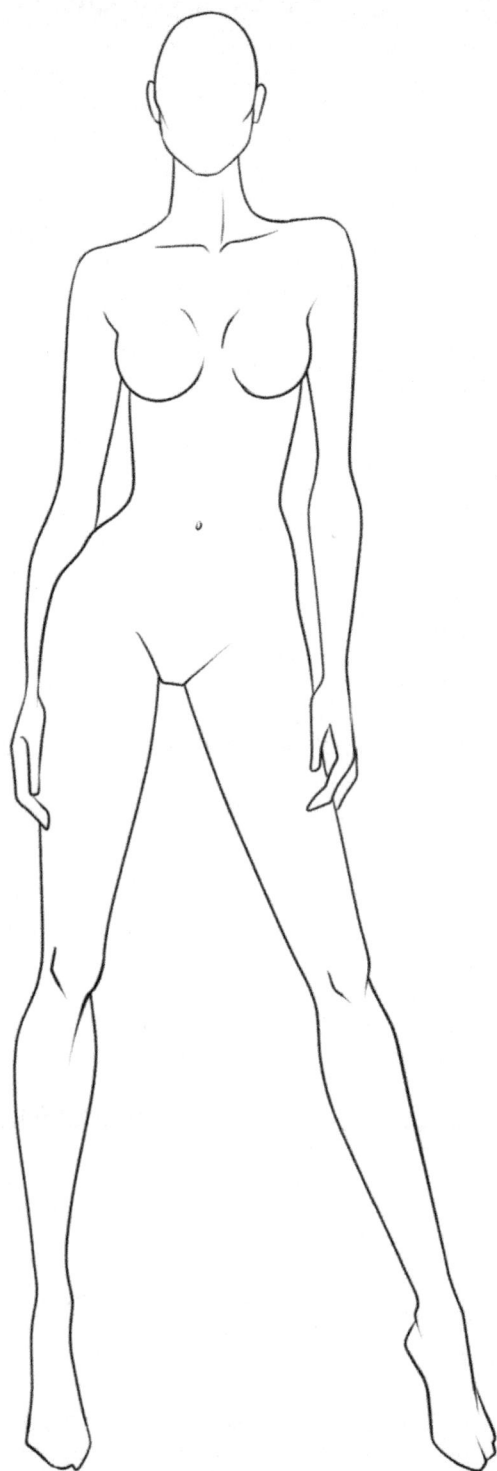

82

WHAT EVENT IS THIS LOOK FOR?

What inspired you for this look?

What kind of materials would you use?

Any other notes describing this look:

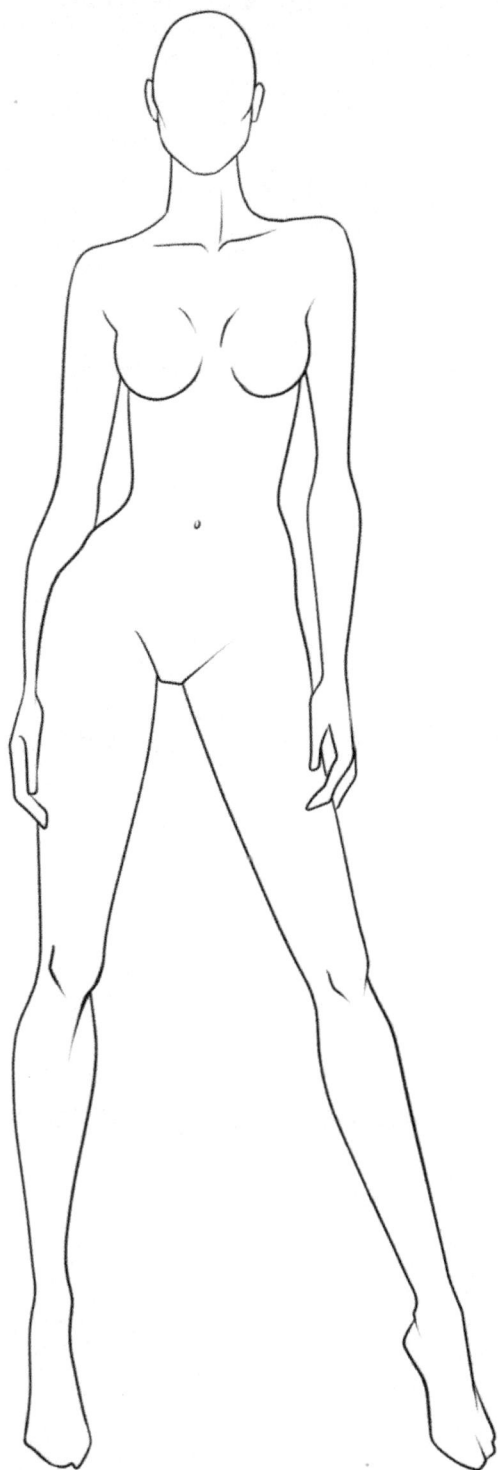

84

WHAT EVENT IS THIS LOOK FOR?

What inspired you for this look?

What kind of materials would you use?

Any other notes describing this look:

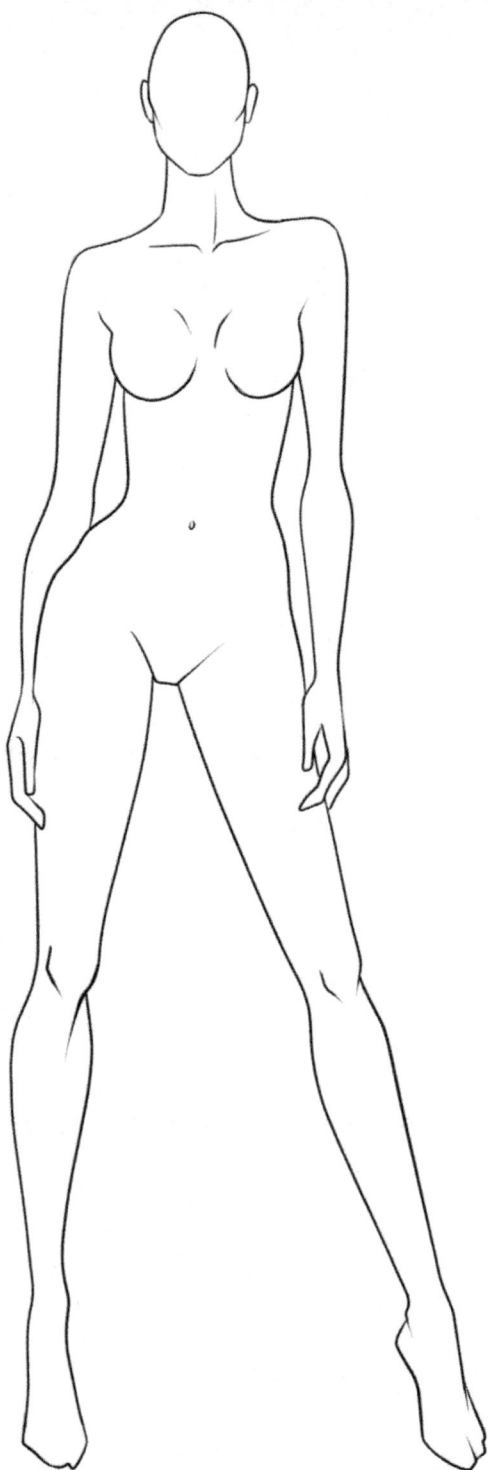

86

WHAT EVENT IS THIS LOOK FOR?

What inspired you for this look?

What kind of materials would you use?

Any other notes describing this look:

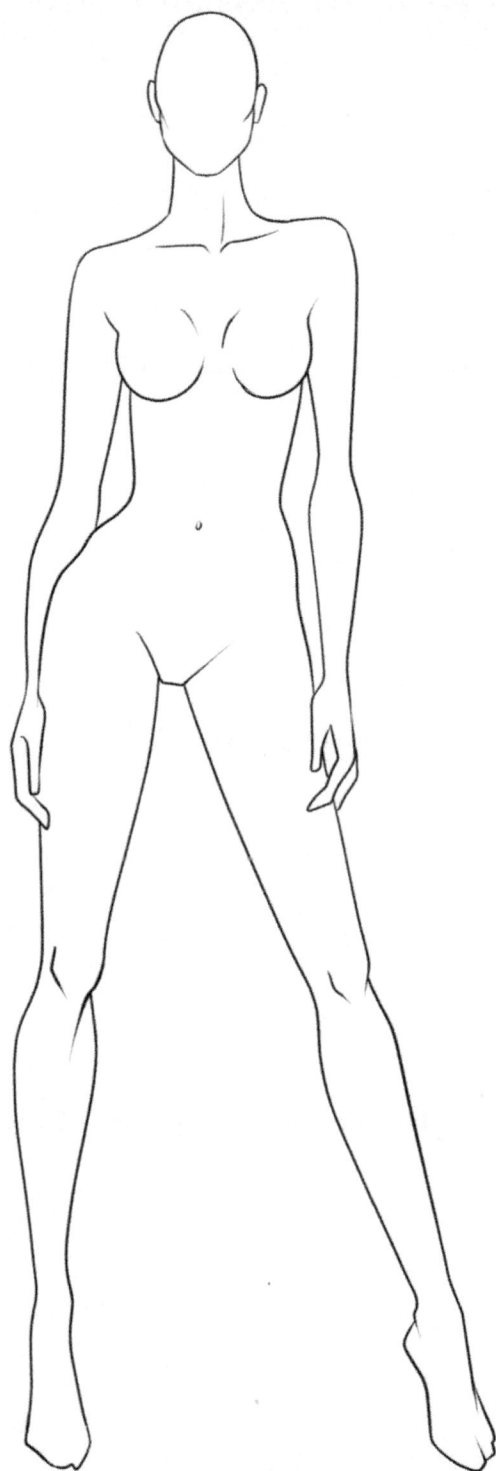

88

WHAT EVENT IS THIS LOOK FOR?

What inspired you for this look?

What kind of materials would you use?

Any other notes describing this look:

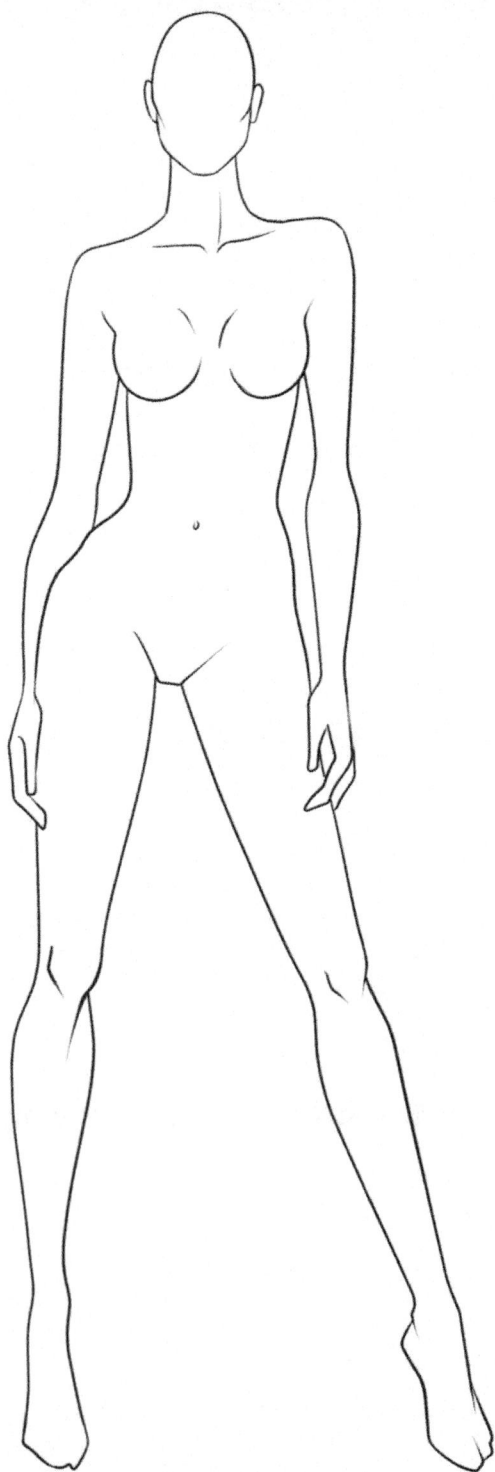

90

WHAT EVENT IS THIS LOOK FOR?

What inspired you for this look?

What kind of materials would you use?

Any other notes describing this look:

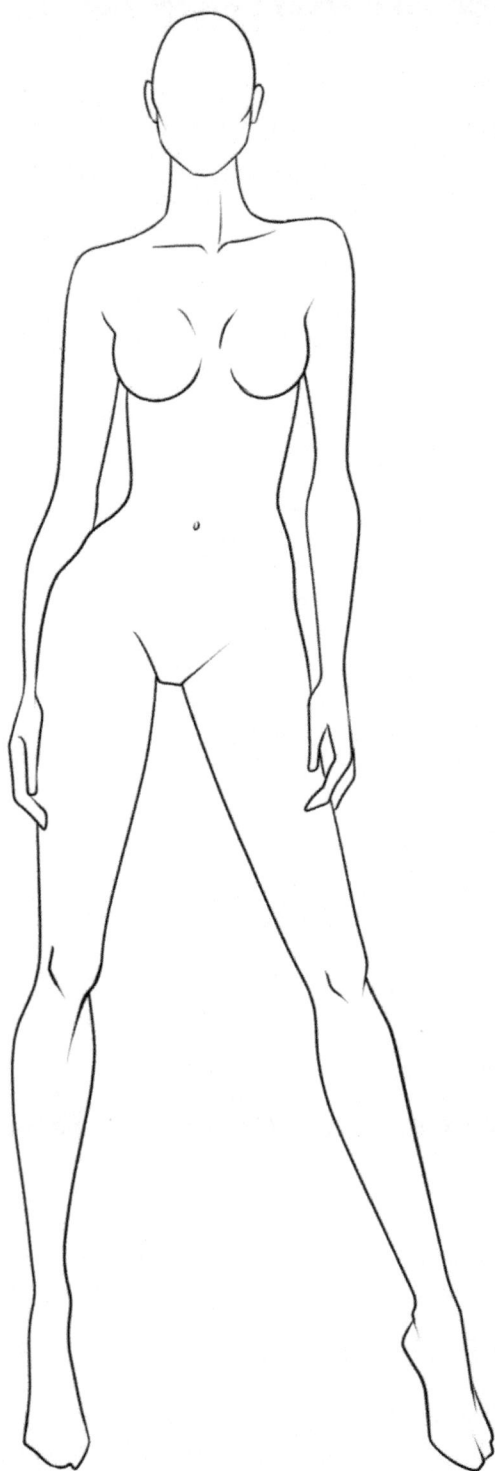

WHAT EVENT IS THIS LOOK FOR?

What inspired you for this look?

What kind of materials would you use?

Any other notes describing this look:

CREATIVE IDEAS

Ever choreographed?

If yes, great. If no, now's the time. Always remember, dancing is about making music visible!

Creativity is
allowing yourself to
make mistakes;
art is knowing which
ones to keep.

TRUST YOUR CREATIVITY

♡

So, no matter how old you are, how experienced you are, what technique you have, you can still create choreography. Dance is just a way of expressing yourself. There is NO such thing as wrong or right within choreographing. Obviously, we can always improve on anything we do, but we are all on different journeys. Creating your own choreography is fun. It's like making your own little piece of art to music. How amazing that the movement you create touches someone and makes someone feel a certain way just by watching? A creative mind always inspires others. However, creativity's worst enemy is self-doubt so just think of creativity as your magic and don't examine it too closely. Let little pieces of your heart go and place them into each project you do.

♡

MUSIC IDEAS

Jot down which songs you would be interested in making up a dance to. (Think what songs make you happy.)

MUSIC IDEAS

Jot down which songs you would be interested in making up a dance to. (Think what songs make you happy.)

MUSIC IDEAS

Jot down which songs you would be interested in making up a dance to. (Think what songs make you happy.)

MUSIC IDEAS

Jot down which songs you would be interested in making up a dance to. (Think what songs make you happy.)

DREAM.
PLAN.
DO.

PLANNING PROJECTS

This section of the book is for you to jot down your ideas and to record any of your choreography plans, so you have it nice and clear in front of you and always have it to refer to.

It's your lucky day; you also have formation grids where you can fill in and mark down the ideas you have using a simple, easy technique.

FOR EXAMPLE:

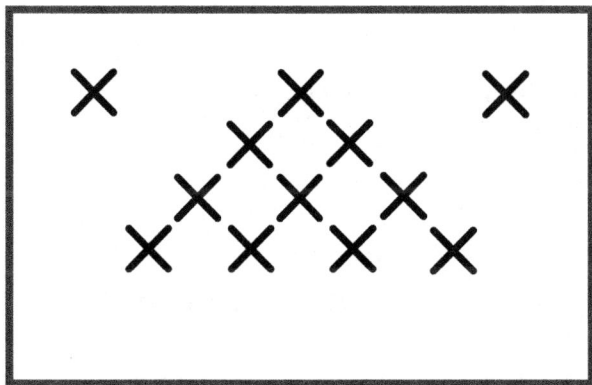

✗ = DANCERS

Go on, get cracking... start to plan, create and have fun.

PLANNING PROJECTS

Name of the piece:

Cast names for project:

What music are you using?

What will this choreography be used for?

What are your intentions and ideas for this piece?

Describe the costumes:

FORMATION GRIDS

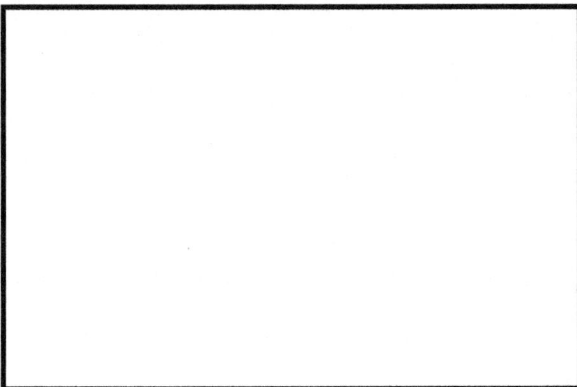

NOTES:

PLANNING PROJECTS

Name of the piece:

Cast names for project:

What music are you using?

What will this choreography be used for?

What are your intentions and ideas for this piece?

Describe the costumes:

FORMATION GRIDS

NOTES:

PLANNING PROJECTS

Name of the piece:

Cast names for project:

What music are you using?

What will this choreography be used for?

What are your intentions and ideas for this piece?

Describe the costumes:

FORMATION GRIDS

NOTES:

PLANNING PROJECTS

Name of the piece:

Cast names for project:

What music are you using?

What will this choreography be used for?

What are your intentions and ideas for this piece?

Describe the costumes:

FORMATION GRIDS

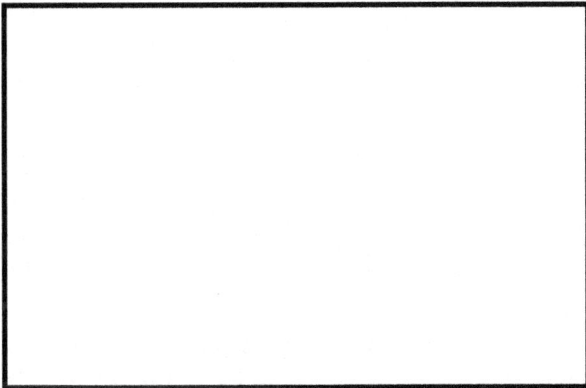

NOTES:

PLANNING PROJECTS

Name of the piece:

Cast names for project:

What music are you using?

What will this choreography be used for?

What are your intentions and ideas for this piece?

Describe the costumes:

FORMATION GRIDS

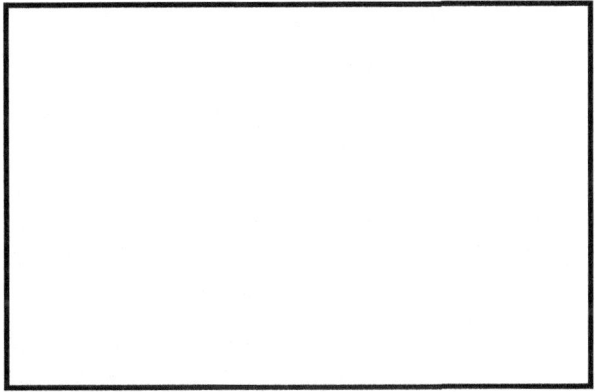

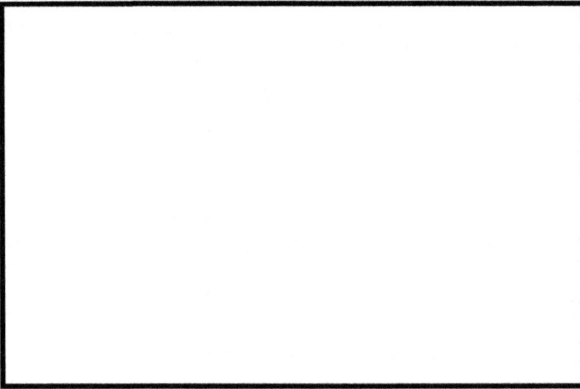

NOTES:

THEME IDEAS

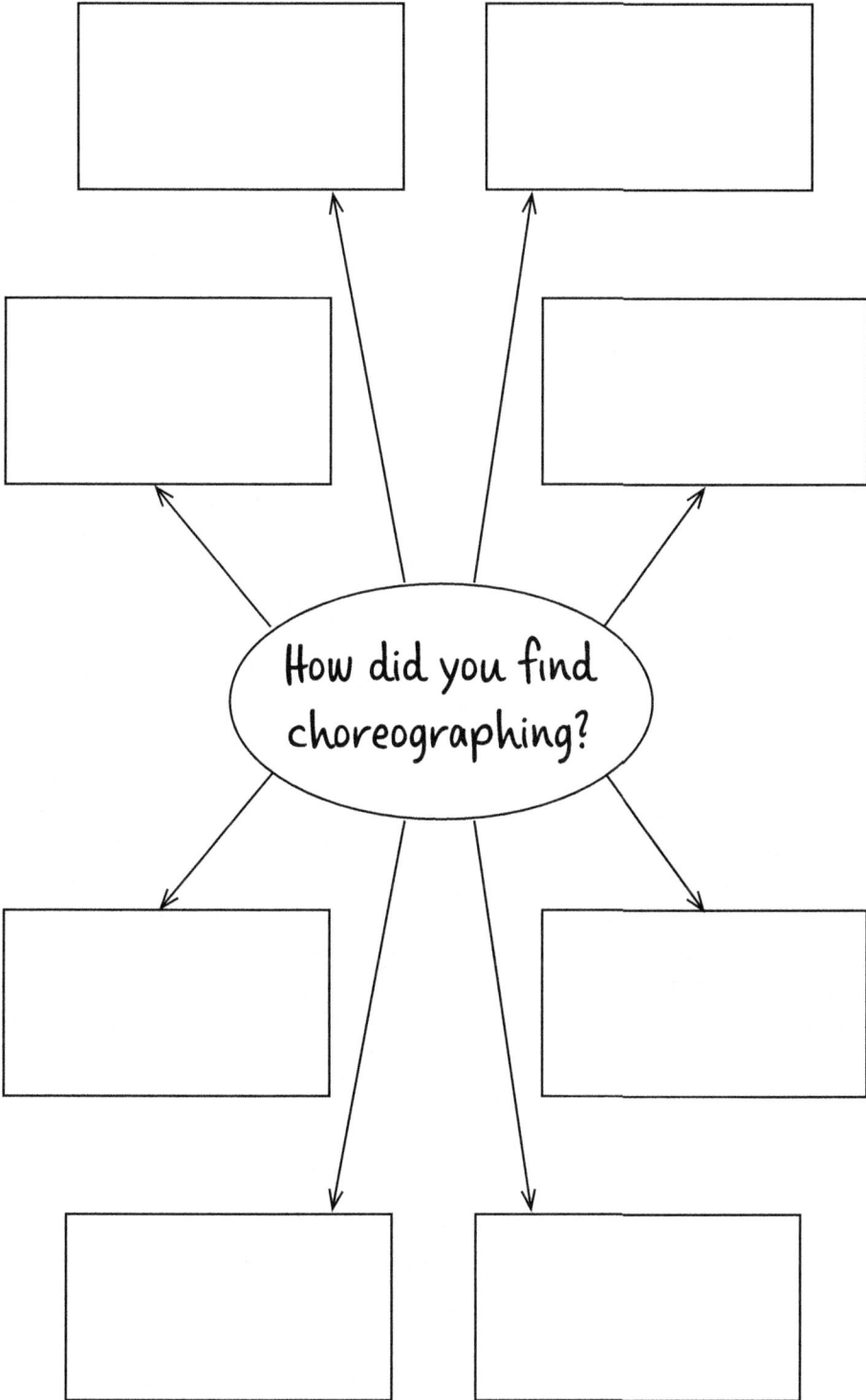

```
┌──────────────┐          ┌──────────────┐
│              │          │              │
│              │          │              │
└──────────────┘          └──────────────┘
         ↑                      ↑
┌──────────────┐          ┌──────────────┐
│              │          │              │
│              │          │              │
└──────────────┘          └──────────────┘
    ↖                              ↗
         ╭─────────────────────╮
         │   How did you find   │
         │   choreographing?    │
         ╰─────────────────────╯
    ↙                              ↘
┌──────────────┐          ┌──────────────┐
│              │          │              │
│              │          │              │
└──────────────┘          └──────────────┘
         ↓                      ↓
┌──────────────┐          ┌──────────────┐
│              │          │              │
│              │          │              │
└──────────────┘          └──────────────┘
```

EXAMS & COMPS

Keep a record of your successes!

Look in the mirror.
That's your competition right there.

EXAM RESULTS

EXAM TYPE	GENRE	RESULTS

EXAM RESULTS

EXAM TYPE	GENRE	RESULTS

COMPETITION SUCCESS

Write down all your proudest competition moments...

MORE
COMPETITION
SUCCESS

Success is achieved and maintained by those who try and keep trying.

NOTES:

HAPPY VIBES

Your own little positivity kit.

Filling in these next couple of pages will remind you of what makes you smile. Oh, and what a fun way to show all the things that make you happy!

BOTTLE UP ONE OF YOUR FAVOURITE MEMORIES AT YOUR DANCE SCHOOL

(Write it in the bottle)

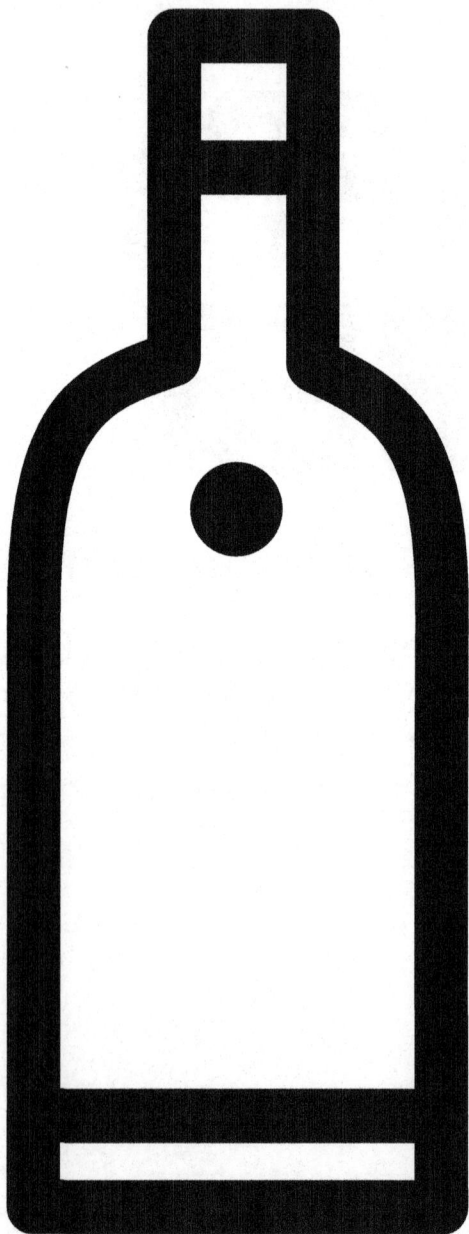

BOTTLE UP ONE OF YOUR FAVOURITE MEMORIES AT YOUR DANCE SCHOOL

(Write it in the bottle)

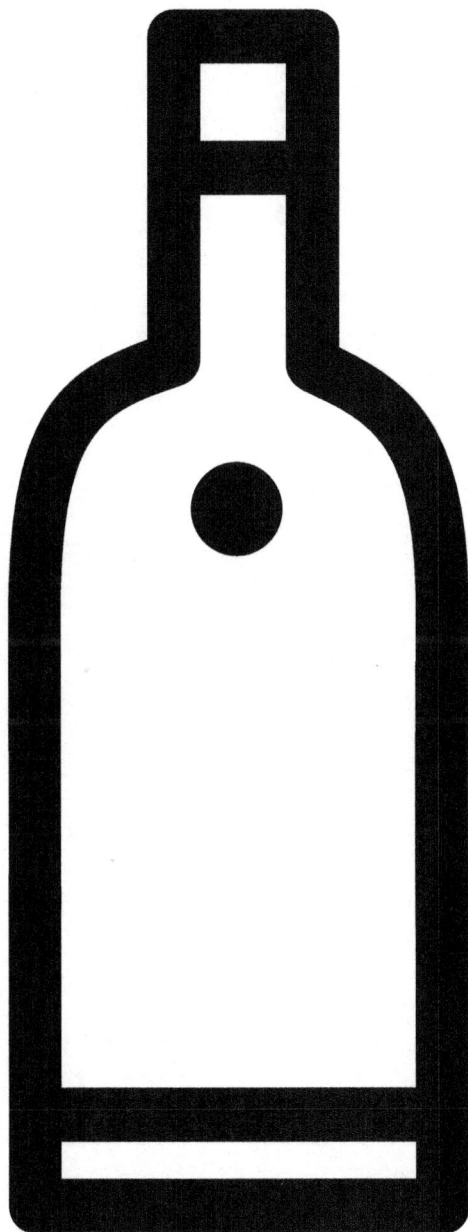

BOTTLE UP ONE OF YOUR FAVOURITE MEMORIES AT YOUR DANCE SCHOOL

(Write it in the bottle)

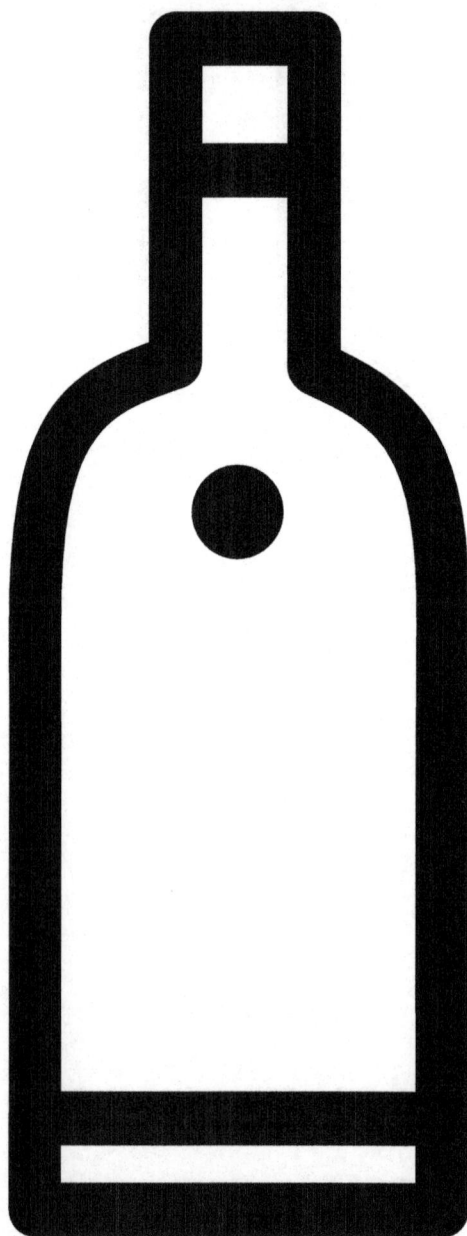

BOTTLE UP ONE OF YOUR FAVOURITE MEMORIES AT YOUR DANCE SCHOOL

(Write it in the bottle)

BEST DANCE TEACHER AWARD

This award goes to:

Congratulations, you were chosen because...

Selfie Time

Draw a selfie with another dancer who makes you happy whenever you see them. It's so important to have support within this industry.

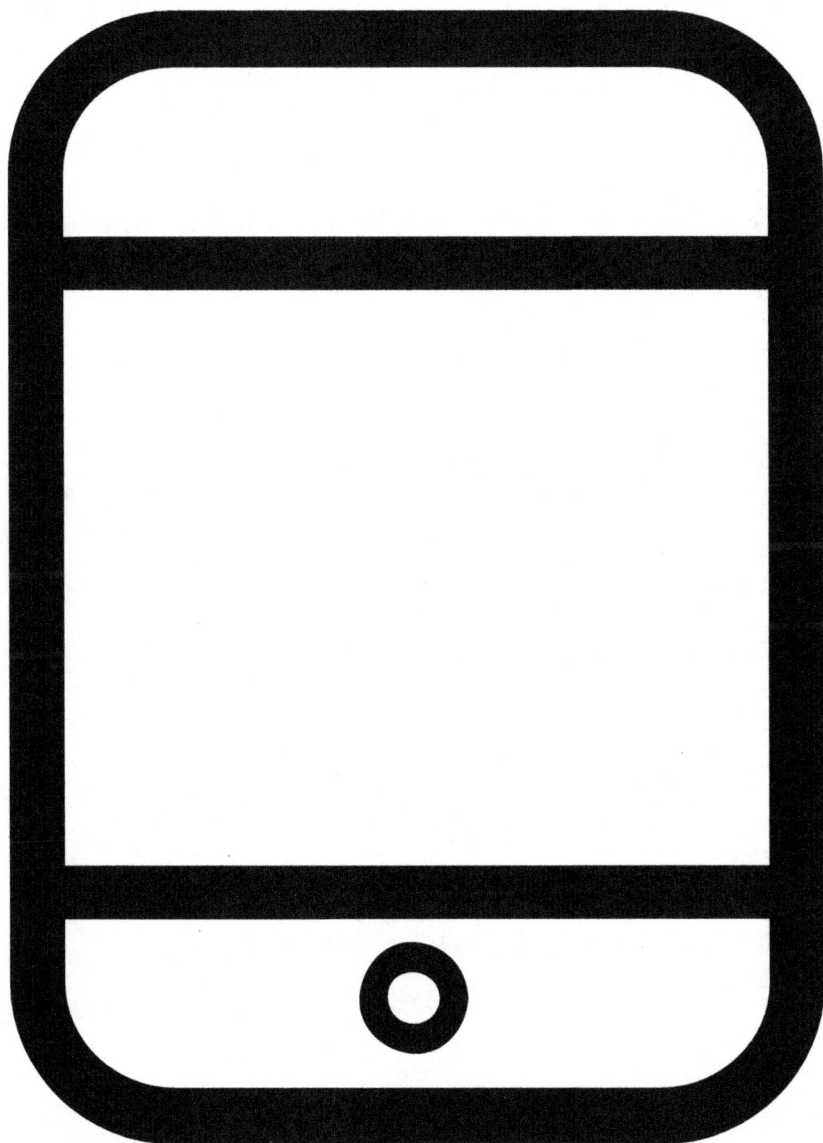

STORYTIME

Fill in the gaps, create your ideal dance day.

Once upon a time, there was a dancer named
.... who dreamed of dancing for .... at
the .... arena in ....! She saw an advert
online that there were auditions at .... studio
in ...., and so it was that she packed her bags
with her best outfits and jumped on a train. She
got through round after round. Every round, she
needed more motivation, so she thought of ....
...................., to remind her to keep it up because she
dreams of being like them.

She didn't need to dream any more, because it
became a reality. Through her hard work and
determination, she went and booked her first
DREAM job. Anything is possible if you put your
mind to it.

And she lived happily ever after.

THE END

WRITE A LETTER TO YOUR SELF FIVE YEARS AGO.
Make yourself smile at how far youv'e come with
your dancing.

Dear...

Yours truly...

What are the nicest compliments you've had?

Fill in the speech bubbles with the best compliments you've had in your dance career...

You can always remember your worth if you ever need cheering up.

I hope this made you smile :)

What are the nicest compliments you've had?

Fill in the speech bubbles with the best compliments you've had in your dance career...

You can always remember your worth if you ever need cheering up.

I hope this made you smile :)

JOT DOWN SOME
MOMENTS OF
PURE HAPPINESS

ESCAPE TO PARADISE

You have just won a ticket to:

Who would you take with you?

What would you take with you?

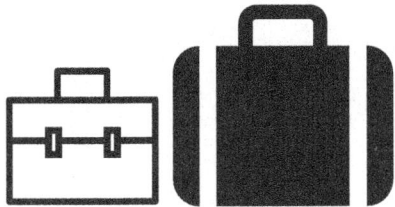

DANCE
LANGUAGE

DESIGN YOUR SELF A MUG WITH A MOTIVATIONAL QUOTE OF YOUR CHOICE

WHAT ARE YOU EXCITED ABOUT?

My Imaginary Audience

Draw the faces of your perfect audience for a performance.

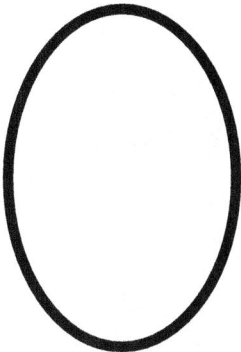

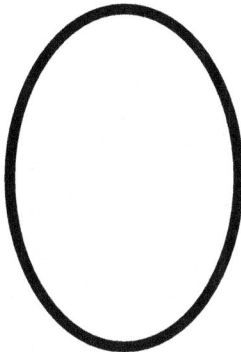

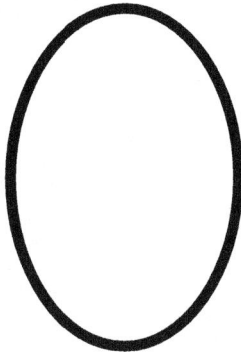

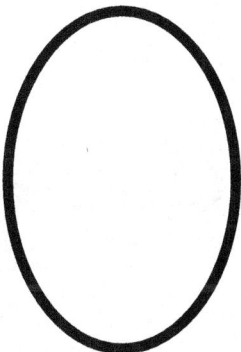

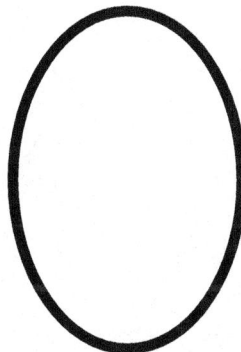

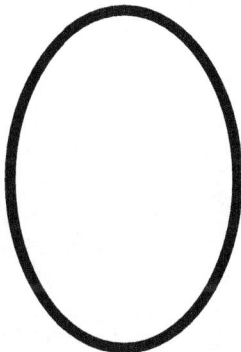

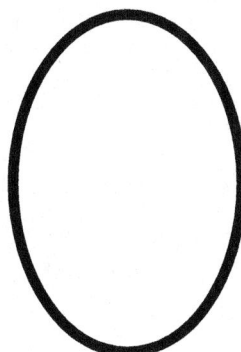

MY DANCE MAP OF HAPPINESS

Mark on the map all the places to do
with dance that make you happy.

PARTY TRICKS

List your 'go to' best dance moves

☆

☆

☆

☆

☆

☆

☆

☆

Gratitude

What are you grateful for?

It's not happiness that brings us gratitude. It's gratitude that brings us happiness, so your first thought every morning should be thank you.

Spend the day appreciating every little joy that comes your way, and you will end up feeling deeply grateful for your life.

Expect nothing, appreciate everything.

Those who have the ability to be grateful are the ones who have the ability to achieve greatness.

Be obsessively grateful.

BESTIE BESTIE

Who's your top dance BFFL?

Stay close to people who feel like sunlight. Someone who brings the best out in you; who makes you laugh and smile. So, if you're always better together, don't let go.

Dance best friends make the good times better and the hard times easier.

Who is your best friend?

Here are a few questions to make your brain start ticking, to help you complete the next few pages...

Who have you made the most wonderful memories with?

Who makes you laugh, uncontrollably?

Who can you trust with your life?

Who is as crazy as you?

Who checks up on you because they genuinely care?

Who would you choose to go on an adventure with?

Have a good think who springs to mind. Then fill in your friend profiles and draw a cute Polaroid of you both, make sure you add colour.

You only can choose five so choose well!

BFFL POLAROID

Name

Age

Favourite colour

Star sign

Favourite dance style

About your friendship

Nickname

What would be your friendship soundtrack? ♪

If you were to make a dance duet act, what would you call it?

How much do you love your dance bestie?!

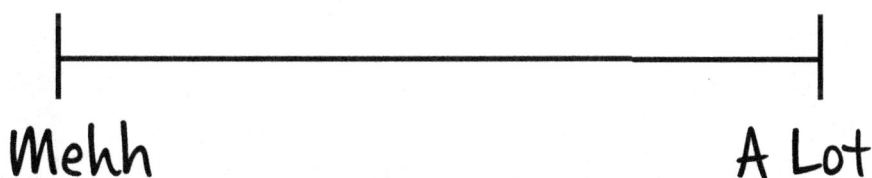

|———————————————————————————|
Mehh   A Lot

What emojis remind you of this bez?

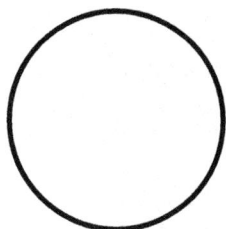

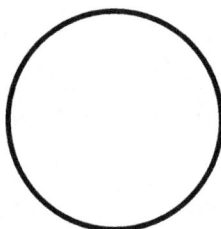

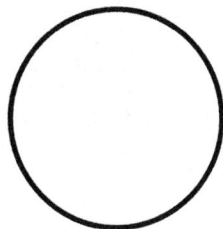

◯   ◯   ◯

BFFL GIFT BASKET

If you had to fill a basket with gifts for this bezzie, what would you fill it with?

FRIENDSHIP
APPRECIATION LETTER

Dear...

Thank you for

You are the bestest friend.
Love

BFFL POLAROID ♥

Name

Age

Favourite colour

Star sign

Favourite dance style

About your friendship

Nickname

What would be your friendship soundtrack? ♪♫

If you were to make a dance duet act, what would you call it?

How much do you love your dance bestie?!

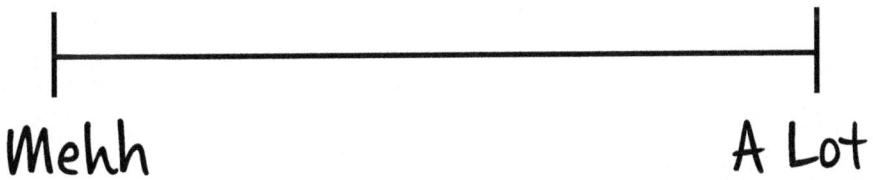

|———————————————————|
Mehh   A Lot

What emojis remind you of this bez?

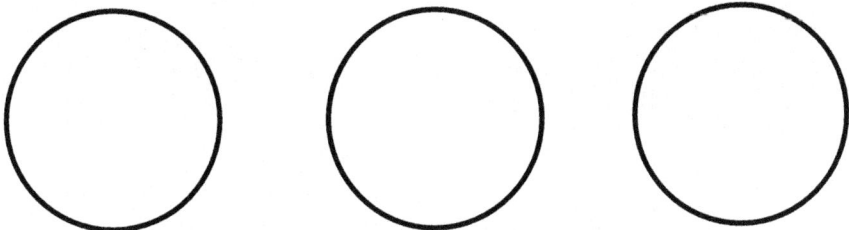

◯ ◯ ◯

BFFL GIFT BASKET

If you had to fill a basket with gifts for this bezzie, what would you fill it with?

FRIENDSHIP
APPRECIATION LETTER

Dear...

Thank you for

You are the bestest friend.
Love

BFFL POLAROID ♥

Name

Age

Favourite colour

Star sign

Favourite dance style

About your friendship

Nickname

What would be your friendship 🎵 soundtrack? 🎵

If you were to make a dance duet act, what would you call it?

How much do you love your dance bestie?!

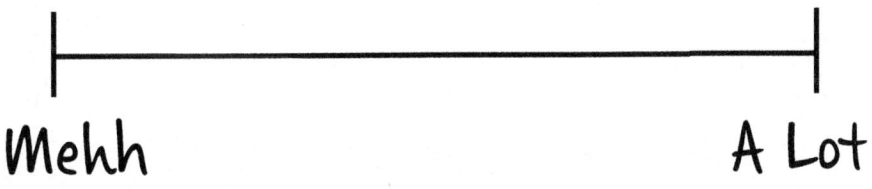

|————————————————————|
Mehh   A Lot

What emojis remind you of this bez?

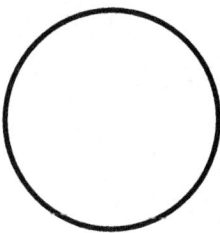

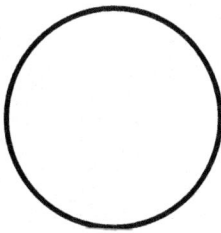

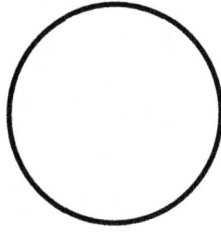

◯   ◯   ◯

BFFL GIFT BASKET

If you had to fill a basket with gifts for this bezzie, what would you fill it with?

FRIENDSHIP
APPRECIATION LETTER

Dear...

Thank you for

You are the bestest friend.
Love

BFFL POLAROID

Name

Age

Favourite colour

Star sign

Favourite dance style

About your friendship

Nickname

What would be your friendship soundtrack? ♫ ♪

If you were to make a dance duet act, what would you call it?

How much do you love your dance bestie?!

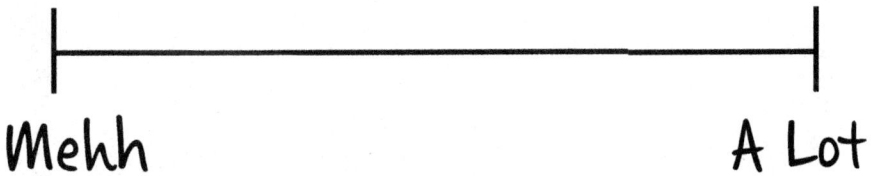

|—————————————————————————————|
Mehh   A Lot

What emojis remind you of this bez?

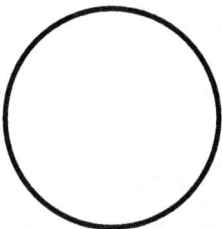

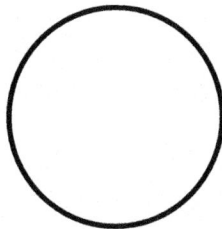

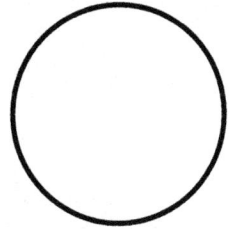

◯ ◯ ◯

BFFL GIFT BASKET

If you had to fill a basket with gifts for this bezzie, what would you fill it with?

FRIENDSHIP
APPRECIATION LETTER

Dear...

Thank you for

You are the bestest friend.
Love

BFFL POLAROID ♥

Name

Age

Favourite colour

Star sign

Favourite dance style

About your friendship

Nickname

What would be your friendship soundtrack?

If you were to make a dance duet act, what would you call it?

How much do you love your dance bestie?!

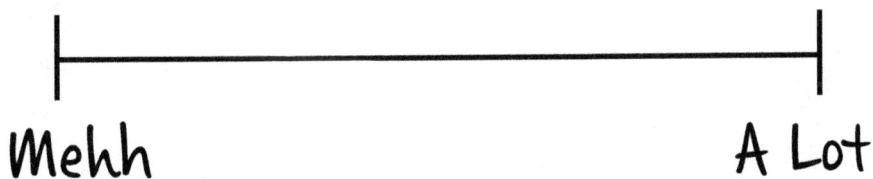

Mehh ———————————————— A Lot

What emojis remind you of this bez?

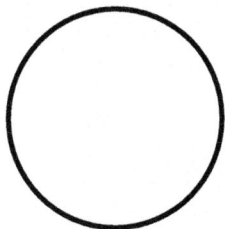

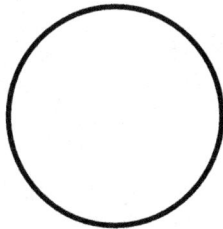

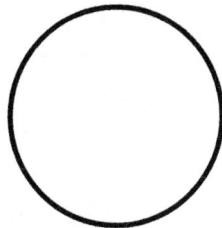

○ ○ ○

BFFL GIFT BASKET

If you had to fill a basket with gifts for this bezzie, what would you fill it with?

FRIENDSHIP
APPRECIATION LETTER

Dear...

Thank you for

You are the bestest friend.
Love

FRIENDSHIP QUIZ

HOW WELL DO YOU KNOW EACH OTHER?
Ask each other these questions and challenge each other.

What's their favourite colour?

Who is one of their favourite dancers?

Who is one of their favourite teachers?

What's one of their dreams?

Can you name their spirit animal?

When is it their birthday?

What's their favourite type of food?

What's one of their favourite shops?
What is their middle name?

What Disney character would they be?

What's their favourite class?

What would they get for their lunch
break at dance?

What's the thing you have in common?

Now go and complement each other :)

DOODLE
PAGE

DOODLE PAGE

DOODLE PAGE

Notes

Peace

Printed in Great Britain
by Amazon